Nellie Bly INVESTIGATES

Written and illustrated by Oliver Brooks

Collins

Before I was known as Nellie Bly, I was born Elizabeth Cochran, in 1864, Pennsylvania, USA.
PINK! It's time to come indoors.
Everybody called me "Pink", because that was the colour of all my clothes.
My father died when I was six, and we suddenly had little money. We moved to a smaller house and couldn't afford my schooling.
When I was 21 years old, I read a newspaper article, called "What Girls Are Good For".
Apparently, all I'm "good for" is bringing up children and feeding my husband.

I wrote an anonymous letter to the editor, criticising the article.
Who is this writer? I'll place an advertisement in the paper.
Your writing is impressive. We want to hire you as a reporter.
I wrote a direct response to that article, called ...
THE GIRL PUZZLE
Let a youth start as an errand boy and he will work his way up until he is one of the firm. Girls are just as smart, and a great deal quicker to learn; why, then, can they not do the same?
Her writing needs work, but she gets her point across.

It was considered "improper" for women to write under their real names, so I chose Nelly Bly, a popular song at the time. However ...
Someone misspelled "Nelly" with an "ie".
From now on, you're "Nellie Bly".
I was determined to highlight the unfair treatment of women in the workplace.
However, my editor made me report on subjects more "appropriate" for a woman journalist, like society parties and gardening.
Mister Madden, you hired me because you liked my voice. Why are you giving me these dull assignments?
Businessmen have complained about your other articles for criticising the conditions in their businesses.
And what does *that* tell you?

Madden agreed to let me travel to Mexico as a foreign correspondent.
Real cowboys!

I was excited to witness a new culture, but was very critical of Mexico's dictator, Porfirio Diaz.

Upon returning to the USA, I was once again writing society articles, so I left to find work in New York.
After an interview with the editor of *The New York World* newspaper, I was given a daring assignment.
We need a woman to go undercover at the asylum on Blackwell's Island. Report only the truth. The good ... and the bad.
The asylum had grown a poor reputation in its treatment of mental health patients.
Err ... yes ... name?
Nellie ... Brown.
Measure her.
Ouch.

Our meals consisted of a thick piece of buttered bread, a bowl of five prunes ...
...and a terrible cup of tea.
– YUCK – It tastes like metal.
Drink up. To have a good brain, the stomach must be cared for.
After dinner, we took our baths, in ice-cold water.

I went to bed with my hair still wet.
It was very cold at night
May I please have a nightgown? It's so cold.
This is a charity. Be thankful for what you get.
I never got much sleep. The night nurses would stomp into the rooms throughout the night.
The blanket was too small.
And when I covered my shoulders, my feet were left freezing.

The next morning, the nurses combed our hair, which had become knotted after the previous night's bath.
Ouch!
Ooh
Ow!
Ahh!
I told one of the medical staff, Dr Ingram, about how cold we were.
Mrs Grady, please give the patients warmer clothing.
Of course, sir. They need only to ask.
If you keep getting us in trouble, Nellie, it will be a serious mistake for you.
Some mornings, visitors would come to look for relatives. One day, I was recognised.
What? Nellie B–
Brown. Nellie Brown. Like Mrs Grady said.
Please, don't give me away.

Many patients didn't need to be there.
Some girls are only here because they don't speak English and the authorities can't understand them.
I told Dr Ingram my concerns over fire safety for the patients.
There are 300 patients locked in rooms. In a fire, you know the staff wouldn't bother unlocking all those doors.
Some prisons can unlock a large number of doors by pulling one handle at the end of a corridor.
I make suggestions, but there is never enough funding to make the changes needed.

The World newspaper released me after ten days. I felt bad leaving my fellow patients behind.

My report encouraged a change in patients' care, including higher budgets for hospitals and more thorough checks before patients are admitted. Its success allowed me to cover other interesting subjects.

I went undercover as a box factory worker to discuss the unfair payment for women ...

... and interviewed a politician on her American presidential campaign.

One Sunday, I was thinking of ideas to present to my editor.
I wish I was on the other side of the world .... Why not? A trip around the world!
I want to try travelling the world as quickly as Phileas Fogg does in Jules Verne's book *Around the World in Eighty Days*!
We've had this idea before, but always intended sending a man.
Besides, a woman needs too much luggage. Only a man can do this.
If you find a man who will do it, then I'll find a paper daring enough to hire me to beat him in the race!

A year later, no one else had agreed to do the trip, so the editor approached me.
I've been thinking ... your idea to travel around the world could bring our newspaper publicity. Could you start the day after tomorrow?
I could start today!
EDITOR

I had to travel light, packing only the essential things for my trip. Writing equipment ... a couple of outfit changes ... toiletries and a drinking flask.
TOOTHPASTE

On 14th November 1889, my trip around the world began.
It's only 28,000 miles before I see my friends again.

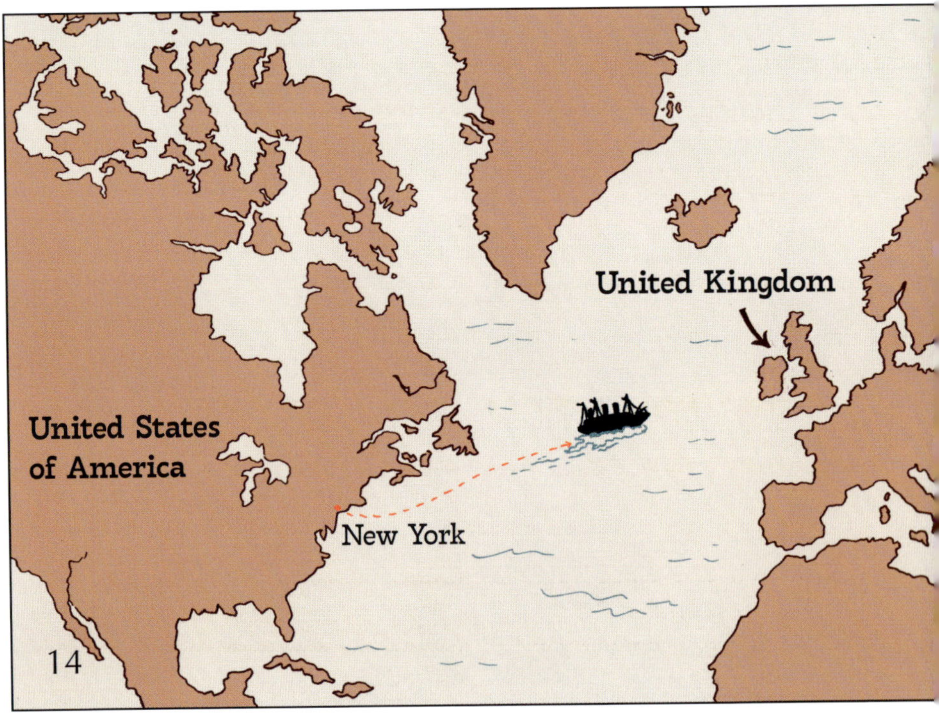
United Kingdom
United States of America
New York

That evening, I was seated at the captain's table for dinner.
It was my first time at sea. As the boat rocked from side-to-side I began to feel seasick.
I went to bed, and was woken the next day by the captain and two passengers.
Thank goodness you're OK – we were worried!
I always sleep late in the morning.
Haha! Morning? It's four in the afternoon.

We docked in the United Kingdom after seven days at sea. As I stepped off the boat, I was met by a reporter from my newspaper's London office.
Jules Verne would like to meet you at his home in Amiens.
In France?
I left for France. It was a slight diversion, but I had to meet the author of the very trip I was attempting.
Mr Verne showed the map he used to plot Phileas Fogg's journey in the book.
If you make the trip in 79 days, I shall applaud you.
I'll do it in 75.

From Amiens, I travelled to another town in France called Calais to catch the train to Brindisi, Italy. From there, I caught a boat to Alexandria in Egypt.
Calais
Amiens
France
Italy
Brindisi
Alexandria
Egypt
My newspaper ran a competition to guess the exact time my journey would take.
First prize is a trip to Europe. I'll guess ... 77 days and 12 hours.
Okay ... 77 days and ... 11 hours.
Nellie Bly is going to experience so many cultures.

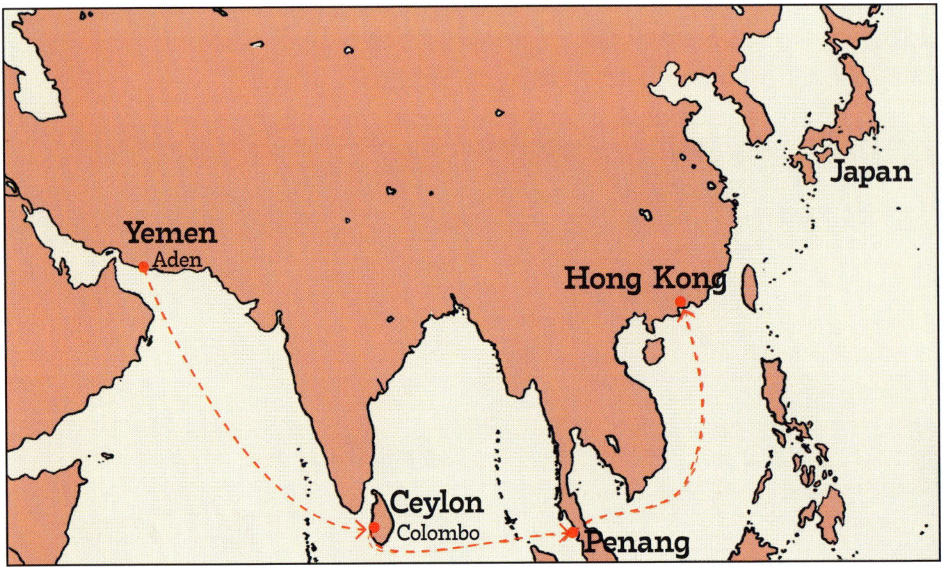
Yemen
Aden
Hong Kong
Japan
Ceylon
Colombo
Penang

We sailed to Yemen, Ceylon (Sri Lanka) and Penang.

Our boat sailed to Hong Kong
in the midst of
a monsoon storm.

This is an incredible journey for a woman to accomplish alone.
But, she doesn't write about the countries she visits. She only cares about the race.

Excuse me, when will the next boat to Japan be?
Of course, Miss ...?
Bly. Nellie Bly.
Nellie Bly? Oh dear. I've heard you're going to lose the race.
I don't think so. I'm making good time.
It's not time that's beating you. It's the other woman ...
... Elizabeth Bisland.

Little did I know, that the editor of *Cosmopolitan Magazine* had hired a reporter to compete against me in the race around the world.
The World
NELLIE BLY TO RACE THE GLOBE
While I had journeyed east, Bisland travelled in the opposite direction, so our paths never crossed.
I promised my editor I will complete the journey in 75 days. If someone wants to do it in less that's their business. I'm not competing.
On New Year's Eve, I sailed to Japan.
HAPPY NEW YEAR
1890

From Japan, I crossed the Pacific on a ship called The Oceanic. Despite the rough weather, I didn't feel seasick this time. Perhaps I had become used to sea travel.
Due to the storm, I landed in San Francisco a day later than expected ...
... however, news of my return spread, and I arrived in Jersey to a cheering crowd. On 25th January 1890, I completed my journey in just 72 days! I felt as though I could hear Jules Verne clapping approvingly.

Elizabeth Bisland finished her journey in 76 days, still beating Verne's calculated time of 80 days.

The person who correctly guessed my time was someone from New York named FW Stevens.

My global exploits brought me great fame.

On 5th April 1895, I retired from writing after marrying industrialist Robert Livingston Seaman.
Robert owned the Iron Clad Manufacturing Company, which produced metal products, such as milk cans and boilers. The company employed 1,500 workers and produced 1,000 cans a day. I took a great interest in the running of the factory and the wellbeing of our employees, learning each of their names.
After nine years of marriage, Robert died and I discovered that somebody had been stealing money from the company.
After many years of legal battles, I was running out of money. In August 1914, I left to seek funds from some friends of mine in Austria, Europe.
I'll only be gone for three weeks.

However, I found that Europe was in the middle of what became known as the First World War.
THE WORLD AT WAR!
Despite having turned 50, I was determined to record scenes from the war. I received a Press Pass from the USA embassy to record life in the trenches.
I travelled with the Austrian Army and, through my articles, encouraged readers at home to send aid to those who were fighting on the front lines.

Those who did not die on the battlefield had to live in pest-filled trenches. I had only planned to stay in Austria for three weeks. I stayed for three years, to make sure readers in America understood the true horrors of this war.

By the time I arrived home, the USA had joined the war against Austria, and my sympathy towards the Austrian soldiers was unwelcome. It was time for me to settle into a quieter life.

In 1919, I began an advice column in the *New York Evening Journal*, answering letters for those in desperate need of help.

Through these letters, I was able to find new homes for abandoned children.

One time, a baby was left in New York's Grand Central Station with a note saying to give him to Nellie Bly at the *Journal,* because they knew I would make sure the baby found a safe home.

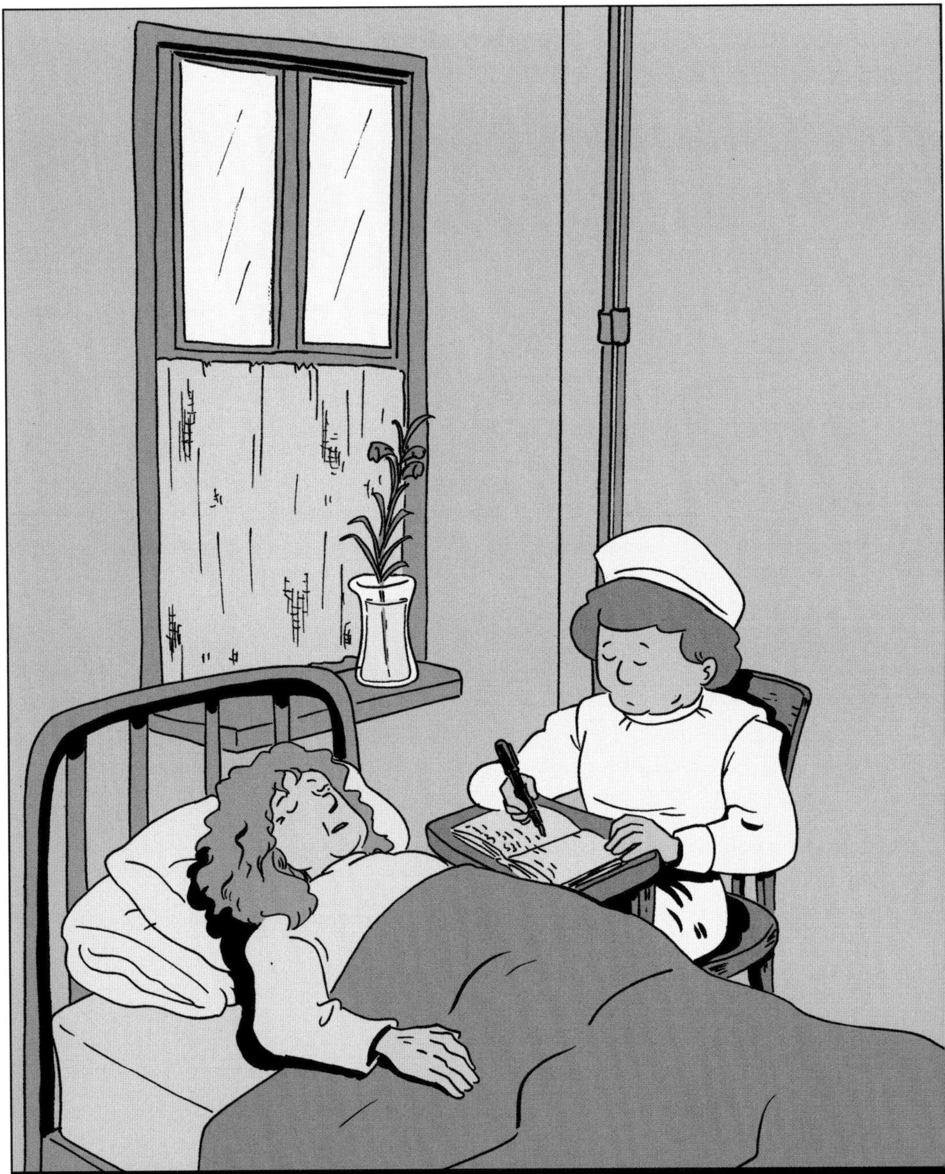

Nellie Bly checked herself into St Mark's Hospital on 9th January 1922, after being unwell with pneumonia. She passed away eighteen days later.

On the northern tip of Roosevelt Island, once called Blackwell's Island, is a collection of statues celebrating women's rights.

Among them, close to the site of the hospital that made her famous, is a statue dedicated to Nellie Bly, called *The Girl Puzzle*. When it opened in 2022, only 8% of statues in the United States were of women. More than a century after her death, Nellie Bly is still making history.

Nellie Bly's Journey

1864 Elizabeth Cochran is born

1885 Becomes a reporter and changes name to Nellie Bly

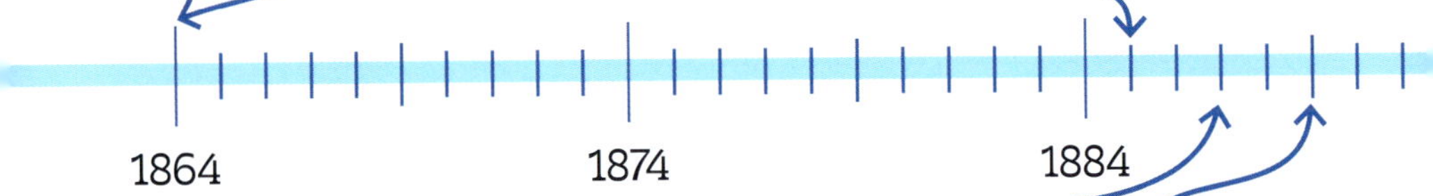

1887 Sent on an undercover assignment at the asylum on Blackwell's Island

1889 Sent on an assignment around the world in under 80 days

1895 Gets married

1914 Travels to Austria. Assignment: Reporting the First World War

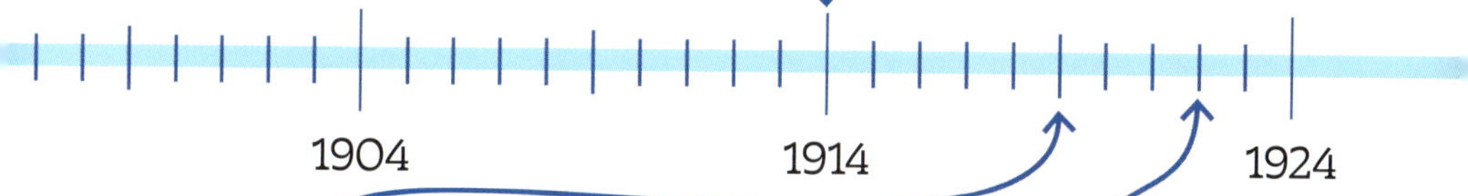

1919 Starts advice column

1922 Nellie Bly dies

Ideas for reading

Written by Gill Matthews
Primary Literacy Consultant

Reading objectives:

- read books that are structured in different ways and read for a range of purposes
- check that the text makes sense to them, discuss their understanding and explain the meaning of words in context
- ask questions to improve their understanding of a text
- retrieve and record information from non-fiction

Spoken language objectives:

- ask relevant questions to extend their understanding and knowledge
- use relevant strategies to build their vocabulary
- articulate and justify answers, arguments and opinions

Curriculum links: Geography: locational knowledge

Interest words: anonymous, criticising, impressive, improper, determined, unfair

Resources: printed world map

Build a context for reading

- Ask children to look at the front cover of the book and to read the title. Discuss what they think the title means.
- Read the back-cover blurb. Ask what they think an investigative reporter might do.
- Point out that this is a biography. Explore what the children think they might find out from the book.

Understand and apply reading strategies

- Ask children to turn to pp2–3. Discuss what they notice about these pages (*that this is a graphic novel*). Ask in which order they would read the boxes. Establish that they would be read left to right and top to bottom.
- Read pp2–5 aloud. Ask children what impression they get of Elizabeth Cochran/Nellie Bly from these pages. Encourage them to support their responses with evidence from the text and the illustrations.